IT'S A NEW DAY
FOR FINANCIAL FREEDOM

BIBLICAL FINANCIAL STUDY

LEADER'S GUIDE

CROWN FINANCIAL MINISTRIES™
True Financial Freedom

CROWN.ORG

ISBN 13: 978-1-56427-232-4

Verses identified as (AMPLIFIED) are taken from the *Amplified® Bible*, © 1954, 1958, 1962, 1964, 1965, 1987 by The Lockman Foundation. Used by permission.

Verses identified as (KJV) are taken from the *King James Version*.

Verses identified as (NIV) are taken from the *Holy Bible: New International Version*, © 1973, 1978, 1984 by the International Bible Society. Used by permission of Zondervan Bible Publishers.

Verses identified as (TLB) are taken from *The Living Bible*, © 1971 by Tyndale House Publishers, Wheaton, Illinois. Used by permission.

All other Scripture quotations are taken from the *New American Standard Bible®* (Updated Edition) (NASB), © 1960, 1962, 1963, 1968, 1971, 1972, 1973, 1975, 1977, 1995 by The Lockman Foundation. Used by permission.

January 2008 Edition

CONTENTS

WELCOME LEADERS!

We are so thankful that you have decided to lead your life group through Crown's *Biblical Financial Study*. God has used the principles in the lives of hundreds of thousands of people who have taken this life group study. We've learned that people benefit most when they are faithful to complete the following.

First of all, before your life group meets, each member should read *Your Money Counts*. This book is easy to read and will provide them with a good overview of the study. Then, they should complete these requirements before each weekly meeting.

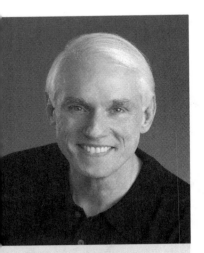

HOWARD DAYTON, CROWN COFOUNDER

1. Homework

Complete the homework in writing. The homework questions are designed to take only about 15 minutes each day to complete. Space is provided in the *Life Group Manual* to answer the questions. If a married couple takes the study together, each will use a separate *Life Group Manual*.

2. Scripture Memory

Memorize an assigned passage from the Bible each week and individually recite the verse(s) at the beginning of the meeting. This will help each participant to remember the most important principles.

3. Practical Application

Complete a practical financial exercise, such as beginning a spending plan or designing a debt repayment plan.

4. Prayer

Everyone prays for the other group members each day. Answers to prayers are one of the most encouraging parts of the life group experience.

> If someone is unable to complete the requirements for a particular week, we ask you, as a leader, not to have him or her participate in that meeting's discussion. This accountability helps us to be faithful. And the more faithful we are, the more benefits we receive from the study.

Attendance. Everyone should attend at least eight of the 10 weekly meetings. Members should notify one of the leaders in advance if they anticipate missing a meeting or arriving late. The meetings are designed to begin and end on time.

Again, we are very grateful you are going to lead the *Biblical Financial Study*. I pray that the Lord will bless you in every way as you share His financial principles.

Howard Dayton, Author
Cofounder, Crown Financial Ministries

PURPOSE

The purpose of the Biblical Financial Study
is to teach people God's financial principles
in order to know Christ more intimately
and to be free to serve Him.

FINANCIAL POLICY

- Crown Financial Ministries does not endorse, recommend, or sell any financial investments. No one may use affiliation with Crown to promote or influence the sale of any financial products or services.

- Crown's *Biblical Financial Study* does not give specific investment advice. No one may use his or her affiliation with Crown to give investment advice.

- Kingdom Advisors, led by Ron Blue and founded by Larry Burkett, is devoted to equipping Christian financial advisors to apply biblical wisdom to their advice and counsel. To learn more about the organization and its Qualified Kingdom Advisor™ designation, please visit KingdomAdvisors.org.

- This study is affordably priced because we do not want cost to be an obstacle to people who desire to participate. If you find the study valuable and want to help make it available to others, you may make a tax-deductible gift to Crown Financial Ministries.

WEB SITE

Crown has designed a Web site as a resource to provide life group members and leaders with up-to-date and detailed financial information. It contains helpful articles, a categorized list of the verses dealing with possessions, links to other useful Web sites, and much more.

Visit the Web site at Crown.org for a world of information.

PERSONAL INFORMATION

A critical ingredient of taking part in a life group study is what happens *after* the study. It is Crown's desire to provide important and useful resources and information that will assist life group members as they walk in the principles they are learning in this study. For us to do this, we need to know who the members are and how to get this information to them.

Please encourage the members to complete the Life Group Member Enrollment Form online in the "My Crown" section of Crown.org. Thank you.

STUDY OBJECTIVES AND LEADER'S RESPONSIBILITIES

Objectives of the Study

1. **Encourage people to experience more intimate fellowship with Christ.**

   Luke 16:11 expresses the correlation between how we handle our resources and the quality of our fellowship with the Lord: *"Therefore if you have not been faithful in the use of worldly* wealth, who will entrust the true riches to you?"*

2. **Challenge each person to invite Jesus Christ to be his or her Lord.**

   We believe money is the primary competitor with Christ for the lordship of our lives. Jesus said, *"No man can serve two masters, you will love one and hate the other. . . . You cannot serve God and Mammon [money]"* (Matthew 6:24).

3. **Build close relationships among the participants.**

4. **Help life group members put their financial house in order.**

The Primary Responsibilities of the Leader

1. **Unconditionally love and encourage the members.**

   People are more receptive to spiritual truth when they have been loved. People want to know how much you care before they care how much you know.

2. **Hold the members accountable.**

3. **Be a model of faithfulness.**

   In Luke 6:40 we read, *"Everyone, after he has been fully trained, will be like his teacher."* Leaders must be faithful to always arrive early, pray consistently for your group members, know the memory verses fluently, and have your homework and practical applications prepared.

4. **Conform to the Crown Financial Ministries' procedure of leading the study.**

---

* The word *worldly* from the *New International Version* has been substituted for the word *unrighteous* from the *New American Standard Bible* to clarify the meaning of this passage.

INFORMATION LEADERS NEED TO KNOW

1. The Leader's Guide

The *Leader's Guide* is divided into three sections:

- Information the leader needs to know
- The weekly homework guides
- The Prayer Logs, Member Evaluation sheet, and Care Log.

2. Practical Application Video

Toward the end of class each week, you will play a segment of the *Practical Application Video*. There are 10 segments of the video—one for each week of the study. For example, at the end of Week 4, play segment 4 of the video.

The *Practical Application Video* explains the next week's assignment and communicates other important information the students need to know. After viewing the video, take time to answer any questions the participants may have. Each life group should have a copy of the *Practical Application Video*.

In addition to the weekly video segments, be sure to use the additional video resources in the "Special Features" section of the DVD to enhance your life group.

3. Group Size

There should be two leaders in each group.

The maximum number of members in a group varies, depending on how many are married couples and how many are individuals. Under no circumstance should there be more than eight. We limit the size of the group because the group dynamic is damaged if the group is too large. The table below will assist you in determining your group size.

Leaders: Co-leaders:	Couple Couple	Couple/Single Couple/Single	Couple/Single Couple/Single	Couple/Single Couple/Single	Single Single
Members:	Couple Couple Couple Couple	Couple Couple Couple Single Single	Couple Couple Single Single Single	Couple Single Single Single Single	Single Single Single Single Single
Totals:	4 Leaders 8 Members	2-4 Leaders 8 Members	2-4 Leaders 7 Members	2-4 Leaders 6 Members	2 Leaders 5 Members

4. Meeting Time

The groups meet for two hours once each week for 10 weeks. The time and day the group meets should be the one most convenient for the participants. Groups may meet anywhere—in homes, offices, or churches. There are couples, men-only, women-only, and mixed groups.

5. Promoting Financial Products and Services

No one may use their affiliation with Crown Financial Ministries to promote or influence the sale of any investments or financial services or professional services.

6. Member Evaluation Sheet

The Member Evaluation sheet is found on page 87 and should be used by the leader to record the performance of the members after each class.

7. Certificate of Achievement

The leaders should award the Certificate of Achievement to the members who have been faithful. They are provided free of charge, and they may be ordered online at Crown.org or by calling 1-800-722-1976.

8. Scheduling the Study

The study is usually conducted three times each year, starting mid-January, the first part of May, and mid-September. However, you may begin a Crown group anytime.

9. More About Crown Financial Ministries®

What is Crown Financial Ministries? Crown is an interdenominational ministry that has developed a comprehensive program to train people of all ages to apply the financial principles from the Bible.

Why is the ministry named Crown? The reason this ministry is named Crown is to remind us to always honor the Lord and serve people.

- Crown Financial Ministries exists to glorify Jesus Christ. He wore a Crown of Thorns when, out of unfathomable love, He died for us (John 19:1-5). Just as the 24 elders in Revelation 4:9-11 cast their crowns before the throne of God, so those serving with Crown should honor Christ in all that we do.

- Crown Financial Ministries exists to serve people. Paul wrote to the Philippians, *"My beloved brothers whom I long to see, my joy and crown"* (Philippians 4:1).

Financial Information: Crown Financial Ministries is a nonprofit, tax-exempt organization governed by a board of directors, none of whom receive a salary from serving on the Crown board. Book royalties are the property of the ministry. Crown is a member of the Evangelical Council for Financial Accountability, whose members must adhere to certain standards, including an annual audit. The ministry is funded primarily by donations, the bulk of which come from graduates of Crown studies, radio listeners, or churches that are implementing Crown programs.

MEMBER ORIENTATION

As the group is being assembled, the leaders should diligently pray that God will bring just the right members into the group. Then the leaders should meet with their members as a group at least two weeks before the study begins. This Member Orientation may be done with only the members of your life group, or there may be a churchwide or citywide orientation.

1. **Start to love the members and build relationships.**

2. **Review the members' requirements by viewing the *Member Orientation Video*.**

   It is located on the *Leader's Training Video*.

   The requirements are designed to take approximately two hours each week outside of class. If for any reason someone comes to the class unprepared, that person will not be allowed to participate in the discussion. The student requirements:

   - Daily homework
   - Scripture to memorize each week
   - Weekly practical application
   - Daily prayer for each participant
   - Attend eight of the 10 classes.

3. **Observe the other important "ground rules."**

   - The class opens and closes in prayer.
   - Scriptures are memorized in the version used in the Crown materials and not in another version of the Bible.
   - The classes start and stop on time.
   - Group discussions are confidential.
   - Students are trained to be future leaders by each person leading one of the weekly meetings.
   - No one will be embarrassed by being required to expose his or her financial situation.

4. **Dispense the materials and collect payment.**

   One member set is required for each person or married couple. A member set for couples contains two *Life Group Manuals*. A member set for an individual contains one *Life Group Manual*. Collect payment from the class.

5. **Encourage all life group members to enroll online.**

   Members should complete the enrollment form online in the "My Crown" section of Crown.org. They will then have access to helpful tools and information to assist them during this study.

6. **Assign the Week 1 homework.**

   The assignment is found on page 8 of the *Life Group Manual* and should be completed prior to attending Week 1. The assignment is to read *Your Money Counts*, memorize Luke 16:11, and answer the homework questions. Ask the members to bring their calendars to the first class to schedule the two socials.

ABOUT THE PRAYER LOGS

To help the participants develop a more consistent prayer life, we utilize the Prayer Log. During the first meeting, ask each person or couple to provide the life group information at the top of the Prayer Log: name and personal information.

- One Prayer Log should be filled out for each person or couple.

- End each class by taking prayer requests from each member or couple. The requests need not be limited to financial concerns. Prior to taking requests, inquire if they have experienced any answers to their prayer requests. There may be more than one request per week.

- To save time, ask the participants to complete their own Prayer Logs before coming to class. Each member is required to pray daily for every member in the group during the 10 weeks. Examine the sample Prayer Log below.

"Pray for one another" (James 5:16).

Name Matt Mitchell   **Spouse** Jennifer

Home phone 422-555-2432   **Children (ages)** John (4), Ruth (3)

Business phone 422-555-8765

Mobile phone 545-555-1239

E-mail mmitchell@wayout.net

Home address 12 Nice Avenue

Pleasantville

Week	Prayer Request(s)	Answers to Prayer
1	John's cold to get better Matt's relationship with boss to improve	
2	Matt's relationship with boss Jennifer's witness to her neighbor	John is completely well
3	Our family faithful to apply God's financial principles	
4	To get out of debt	Matt had an encouraging talk with his boss
5	For the boat to sell soon	

LOVING THE MEMBERS

1. Love your life group members outside of class.

Care Log. The purpose of the Care Log is to ensure that the leaders contact their life group members each week to encourage and love them. The weekly contacts may be by telephone, mail, e-mail, or in person. The two leaders should alternate each week in their responsibility to contact the members by deciding who will contact them on the odd-numbered weeks and who will contact them on the even-numbered weeks.

The members should *not* be aware of the Care Log. The leaders should inspect each other's Care Logs weekly to encourage faithfulness.

Week	Initials of leader responsible for contact	R. Jones	J. Morgan	M/M Mitchell	M. Turner	B. Hunt			
				LIFE GROUP MEMBERS					
1	JC	Phone 1/13	Lunch 1/14	Phone 1/13	Postcard 1/16	Phone 1/13			
2	TM	Phone 1/20	Phone 1/20	Saw in person	Phone 1/22	Card 1/21			
3	JC								

Socials. The leaders should organize two social events for the life group. These activities may be for a dessert, a meal, or any other relaxed setting that will encourage the development of relationships. The first social should be scheduled midway through the study. The second social should be held as soon as possible after the study. It is also a good idea to visit the members where they work or live.

2. Love your students inside of class.

The leader's attitude should be loving, humble, and caring—not a critical or a know-it-all attitude. We are "students-among-students"; we all are growing in understanding the unfathomable Word of God.

After a member answers a question, encourage, affirm, and thank him or her. If an answer is incorrect, be careful not to discourage the member by responding harshly or negatively. Maintain good eye contact and be attentive, because we communicate through our body language.

1. **Open with prayer. We recommend that you pray on your knees.**

2. **Individually recite the Scripture to memorize.**

3. **Confirm that the Practical Applications have been completed.**

4. **Conduct the group discussion. The discussion should proceed as follows:**
   - Different group members read the Scriptures for a particular day's homework.
   - Proceed in a circle, asking every person to answer all the questions for that day's homework. If the answer to a question is obvious, it is not necessary for more than one person to answer the question.
   - In a couples group, everyone should answer the Day One Homework. Then the men and women should alternate in answering the questions for Days Two through Six Homework.

5. **Complete the items listed in the Remaining Agenda in consecutive order.**

6. **View the *Practical Application Video*.**

7. **Share prayer requests and write them in the Prayer Logs.**

8. **End in prayer.**

Small Group Dynamics

- In Diagram 1 the sole focus is on the leader who does all the talking. The participants are passive. This is not how Crown life groups are designed.

- Diagram 2 reflects a group interacting with one another and a leader who guides and facilitates the discussion. The leader must establish an environment in which members have the freedom to express their insights and questions.

DIAGRAM 1
The Wrong Method

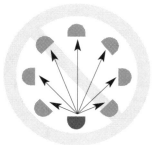

Leader

DIAGRAM 2
The Correct Method

Leader

HOW TO SELECT AND TRAIN LEADERS FROM AMONG YOUR LIFE GROUP MEMBERS

1. **Set the Stage**

   In the member orientation, tell your group that you are going to train them to be leaders. Whether they become leaders depends on their desire to lead the study and their faithfulness during the study.

2. **Test the Members**

   The most experienced leader should lead weeks one and two. The co-leader should lead weeks three and four. Then each member should be invited to lead one or two of the weeks.

   As a life group leader, you need to make sure that group members have access to the Leader's Guide for the week they are leading. You may let them borrow your Leader's Guide or, if you prefer, you are permitted to make a copy of individual weeks as necessary for this exercise.

3. **Selection of Leaders**

   You should consider only the members who are faithful during the study.

4. **Validation of Leaders**

   Any potential leader should be approved by the church leadership if the study is conducted within a church.

5. **Invitation of Leaders**

   After a person has been selected and validated as a leader, invite that person to lead the study. If he or she decides to become a leader, that person needs to be trained.

6. **Training of Leaders**

   For your life group members to be qualified to lead the study, they should do the following.

   - Study the Leader's Guide.
   - Complete a training session during which they view the *Leader's Training Video*. This training session may be conducted by a church or in a citywide event, or it may be via self-study online at Crown.org.

HOW TO BEGIN THE CROWN PROGRAM IN THE CHURCH

An explanation of how to begin a Crown financial teaching ministry in a church is described in detail in the Crown *Church Manual*. The following is an abbreviated outline of the steps.

1. **Introduce Crown Financial Ministries to the pastor/church leadership.**

   Meet with the pastor and appropriate church leadership to explain the program. The Introduction Video is very helpful in describing the program. This video is located on the *Leader's Training Video*. To successfully implement the study in a church, it is essential to have the active support of the church leadership.

2. **Select and train the life group leaders.**

   The number of people that will need to be trained is determined by the number of groups the church wants to begin.

3. **Select the students for the initial group or groups.**

   The major objectives of the initial groups are to multiply the number of people qualified to lead and to enable some of the church leadership to experience the study.

4. **Choose the initial church coordinator.**

   The church coordinator (usually a layperson) has the overall responsibility of implementing Crown Teaching Solutions within the church. This position requires a commitment of time and effort and should be the person's primary, if not sole, ministry. The pastor should be involved in the selection process. The first person serving in this role is often gifted as an initiator but will want to be replaced in a year or two.

5. **When Crown is opened to the church.**

   - Bathe every presentation in prayer, asking God to motivate the life group members He wants in the study.

   - Communicate the content and benefits of the study, and never use any hard-sell tactics. Describe the requirements and accountability and the need to invest two hours of preparation each week outside of class.

   - Churches have used several methods to present the study: a life group member's personal recommendation to a friend, the pastor's recommendation from the pulpit, testimonies from Crown life group members in front of the church, an announcement in the church handout, and using the Introduction Video. This video is located on the *Leader's Training Video*.

LEADER'S CHECKLIST

There are four elements a leader must put in place to build a successful life group study.

1. **The leader must love the members.**

2. **The leader must hold the members accountable.**

3. **The leader must model faithfulness.**

4. **The leader must conduct the study according to the Crown Financial Ministries procedure.**

We want to serve you and help you maintain a standard of excellence. In order to assist you, an experienced Crown life group leader may visit your group. After the class has ended and the members have departed, the experienced leader will meet with you to discuss the class and answer any questions. This is the checklist that will be used as a guide.

1. **Describe how the leaders loved the members.**

2. **Did the leaders hold the members accountable to fulfill their responsibilities?**
   - ❏ Scripture Memory
   - ❏ Homework
   - ❏ Practical Application
   - ❏ Daily Prayer

3. **Did the leaders model faithfulness in the following areas?**
   - ❏ Scripture Memory
   - ❏ Homework
   - ❏ Member Evaluation Sheet
   - ❏ Practical Application
   - ❏ Daily Prayer
   - ❏ Care Log/Two Socials Scheduled

4. **Did the leaders conduct the study according to the Crown Financial Ministries agenda?**
   - ❏ Start on Time
   - ❏ Opening Prayer
   - ❏ Scripture Memory
   - ❏ Confirm Practical Application
   - ❏ Correctly Lead Discussion
   - ❏ View Practical Application Video
   - ❏ Prayer Requests
   - ❏ Ending Prayer / Stop on Time

Additional Comments:

PLACES TO SERVE

If you have a desire to help others learn God's way of handling money, there are four places you can serve with Crown as illustrated in the baseball diamond.

1. Serving Individuals.

The heroes of Crown Financial Ministries are the life group leaders and Money Map coaches, because the life group and one-on-one are where life changes take place.

2. Serving the Church.

If you want to impact your entire church, you may serve as the church coordinator or on the church team.

3. Serving Your City.

If you have a desire to influence your community, third base is for those who serve as an area director or on the city team. And in order for Crown to have a broad impact on a larger city, it is necessary to have a full-time city director and a functioning team of volunteers.

4. Serving Beyond the City.

"Home plate" is for those who have a "missionary spirit" and wish to help introduce Crown to other cities and even other countries. If you wish to serve your church, or your city, or even beyond your city, visit the "Volunteering" section of Crown.org for more information on these positions.

The Next Step

1. What I need to do to begin my first group:

- My leader or co-leader is . . .
- My potential life group members are . . .

    (Concentrate on selecting members who have the potential to become future life group leaders. It is also helpful to have someone representing the church leadership participate.)

- Describe how you will ask the members to participate.
- Describe how you will schedule the Member Orientation.
- My goal is to start my first group by this date:

2. What I need to do to help Crown grow in my church:

- Meet with my pastor/church leadership to discuss Crown Financial Ministries.
- The acting Crown church coordinator is . . .
- Those who will serve on the initial church team are . . .

How we handle money impacts our relationship with the Lord.

CROWN'S OVERVIEW OF WEEK 1: The primary objectives for Week 1 are to begin to develop close relationships among the participants and to reinforce the study requirements. Leaders should have read the Introduction Notes on pages 10-11 in the *Life Group Manual* before class.

NOTE: The blank space following each agenda number is for the leader to fill in the scheduled time for each agenda item. For example, if your class begins at 7:00, #1 would read at 7:00, #2 would read at 7:05, #3 would read at 7:10, and so forth. This is designed to assist the leader in monitoring the time so that the class will end punctually.

AGENDA

1. _____ (5 minutes) **Open in prayer.**

2. _____ (5 minutes) **Each person individually recites from memory Luke 16:11.**
   "Therefore if you have not been faithful in the use of worldly* wealth, who will entrust the true riches to you?"

3. _____ (5 minutes) **Ask the students if they have completed their online Life Group Member Enrollment Form in the "My Crown" section of Crown.org. This membership provides free tools and resources to enhance their life group experience. Also, review the requirements found on page 4 of the *Life Group Manual*.**

4. _____ (70 minutes) **Ask everyone to introduce themselves, beginning with a leader. Ask them to share how they were introduced to Jesus Christ, what they do for a living, and something about their families. To determine how much time each person is allotted, divide the number of people into 70 minutes. The leaders should communicate this time constraint. If a member is too brief, the leader should gently ask additional questions to provide the member with an opportunity to express himself or herself more fully.**

5. _____ (10 minutes) **Begin the homework discussion.**

* The word *worldly* from the New International Version has been substituted for the word *unrighteous* from the New American Standard Version to clarify the meaning of this passage.

REMINDER FOR LEADERS: Remember to enroll online as a Life Group Leader in the "My Crown" section of Crown.org. After enrolling, you can input your life group members' e-mail addresses so that you can easily communicate with them on a weekly basis.

After getting your Group Code, please write it down here and tell your group so they can join.

My Group Code: _____

INTRO

Scripture to Memorize

"Therefore if you have not been faithful in the use of worldly* wealth, who will entrust the true riches to you?"
(Luke 16:11).

* The word *worldly* from the New International Version has been substituted for the word *unrighteous* from the *New American Standard Bible* to clarify the meaning of this passage.

Practical Application

In addition to memorizing the Scripture above and completing the Homework below, read *Your Money Counts* prior to the first meeting. Please fill out your life group member enrollment form online at Crown.org. On the *Crown Money Map,*™ review the definition of "True Financial Freedom" and complete the "My Life Purpose" section.

Homework

1. What was the most helpful information you learned from reading *Your Money Counts*?

Read Isaiah 55:8-9.

2. Based on this passage, do you think God's financial principles will differ from how most people handle money? What do you think would be the greatest difference?

> **NOTE TO LEADER:** Crown's comments, enclosed in brackets, will follow each question. Following Crown's comments there will be space for the leader's response to the question.

[God's economy operates on entirely different principles. Most people do not believe He plays a role in finances, but Scripture reveals He has the dominant role.]

Read Luke 16:11.

3. What does this verse communicate to you about the importance of managing possessions faithfully?

[How we handle money affects our fellowship with Christ.]

4. How does handling money impact our fellowship with the Lord?

[If we are unfaithful with money, our fellowship with God will suffer.]

Scripture memory helps

The memory verses cards are found in the back of the *Practical Application Workbook* and are designed to be removed and carried with you throughout the day.

REMAINING AGENDA

1. _____ (5 minutes) **Play the Week 1 segment of the *Practical Application Video,* which reviews what the members are required to do for next week**.

   - Read the Introduction Notes on pages 10 and 11 in the *Life Group Manual.*

   - Complete the God's Part and Our Part Homework on pages 14-17 in the *Life Group Manual.*

   - Complete the Personal Financial Statement, begin recording Income and Spending, prepare the Quit Claim Deed on page 14 in the *Practical Application Workbook,* and review the My Life Goals samples. Also, locate where you are on the *Crown Money Map™* and review Destination 1.

2. _____ (5 minutes) **After viewing the Week 1 segment of the *Practical Application Video,* answer any questions the members have about next week's assignment.**

   - **REVIEW THE CALENDAR** to determine if any regularly scheduled classes fall on a holiday. If there are any conflicts, please reschedule at this meeting.

   - **SCHEDULE THE TWO SOCIALS.**

   - **COMPLETE THE PRAYER LOGS.** Participants should have one Prayer Log for each person or couple, including himself or herself.

3. _____ (10 minutes) **Take prayer requests and note them in the Prayer Log.**

4. _____ (5 minutes) **End in prayer.**

REMINDER FOR LEADERS: Complete the members' evaluations on page 87. Decide which leader will be responsible for what week on the Care Log. Be sure to contact each member this week by logging in to the "My Crown" section of Crown.org and sending them an e-mail or digital post card. Encourage members who have not already done so to complete their online enrollment form at Crown.org.

The Lord is Owner of all.

CROWN'S OVERVIEW OF WEEK 2: The primary objective for Week 2 is to estabish in the life group members' hearts and minds that God is preeminent over all of life, including the areas of money and possessions. Leaders should have read the God's Part and Our Part Notes on pages 18-25 in the *Life Group Manual* before class.

AGENDA

1. _____ (5 minutes) **Open in prayer.**

2. _____ (5 minutes) **Each person individually recites from memory 1 Chronicles 29:11-12, TLB.**

   "Everything in the heavens and earth is yours, O Lord, and this is your kingdom. We adore you as being in control of everything. Riches and honor come from you alone, and you are the Ruler of all mankind; your hand controls power and might, and it is at your discretion that men are made great and given strength."

3. _____ (5 minutes) **Confirm that members have completed the Personal Financial Statement practical application, have started the Recording Income and Spending worksheet, have completed the Quit Claim Deed, have reviewed the My Life Goals samples, and have located where they are on the *Crown Money Map*™ and reviewed Destination 1. Ask the members to have their completed deeds witnessed by others in the group. Answer any questions concerning the practical applications.**

4. _____ (80 minutes) **Begin the group discussion.**

REMINDER FOR LEADERS: The discussion for each day's homework should proceed as follows. **(1)** Read the Scriptures. Assign one passage of Scripture from that day's homework to each person to read (as far as the verses will go). **(2)** Proceed in a circle, asking each person to answer all the questions for that day's homework. For example, "Bob, how did you answer the questions for day three?" If the answer to a question is obvious, it is not necessary for more than one person to answer the question. If you are running out of time, ask the members to be brief in their responses.

Scripture to Memorize

"Everything in the heavens and earth is yours, O Lord, and this is your kingdom. We adore you as being in control of everything. Riches and honor come from you alone, and you are the Ruler of all mankind; your hand controls power and might and it is at your discretion that men are made great and given strength" (1 Chronicles 29:11-12, TLB).

Practical Application

Complete the Personal Financial Statement, begin keeping a record of everything you spend, and complete the Quit Claim Deed (bring it to class to be witnessed by members of your group). Find your location on the *Crown Money Map*™ and also review Destination 1.

Day One - Let's Review the Introduction

Read the Introduction Notes on pages 10-11 and answer:

1. What information especially interested you?

   [Emphasize that how we handle money affects our fellowship with Christ.]

2. Comment on any personal challenges you felt after learning the three reasons the Bible says so much about money.

GOD'S PART AND OUR PART

Day Two

Read Deuteronomy 10:14; Psalm 24:1; and 1 Corinthians 10:26.

1. What do these passages teach about the ownership of your possessions?

   [The Lord owns everything in the world.]

Read Leviticus 25:23; Psalm 50:10-12; and Haggai 2:8.

2. What are some of the specific items that God owns?

   Leviticus 25:23 - [**God owns all the land.**]

   Psalm 50:10-12 - [**God owns all the animals.**]

   Haggai 2:8 - [**God owns all the gold and silver.**]

3. Prayerfully evaluate your attitude of ownership toward your possessions. Do you consistently recognize the true owner of those possessions? Give two practical suggestions to help recognize God's ownership.

   [**Consider altering your vocabulary by dropping the possessive pronouns ("my," "mine," and "ours") and substituting "His" or "the" instead. For 30 days, each morning and night, meditate and prayerfully recite 1 Chronicles 29:11-12.**]

Day Three

Read 1 Chronicles 29:11-12 and Psalm 135:6.

1. What do these verses say about God's control of circumstances?

   [**The Lord is in control of all circumstances.**]

Read Proverbs 21:1; Isaiah 40:21-24; and Acts 17:26.

2. What do these passages tell you about God's control of people?

   Proverbs 21:1 - [**God controls the heart of each person.**]

   Isaiah 40:21-24 - [**The Lord is in absolute control of all people.**]

   Acts 17:26 - [**The Lord controls the boundaries and duration of every nation.**]

3. Do you normally recognize the Lord's control of all events? If not, how can you become more consistent in recognizing His control?

LEADER—you should have approximately **one hour** of class time remaining. We recommend a three-minute stretch break for your group at this time.

Day Four

Read Genesis 45:4-8; Genesis 50:19-20; and Romans 8:28.

1. Why is it important to realize that God controls and uses even difficult circumstances for good in the life of a godly person?

   [God works every circumstance for good in the life of those who love Him and are yielded to Him as Lord. Joseph suffered difficult circumstances, but God orchestrated those difficulties for ultimate good.]

2. How does this perspective impact you today?

3. Share a difficult circumstance you have experienced and how God ultimately used it for good in your life.

Day Five

Read Psalm 34:9-10; Matthew 6:31-33; and Philippians 4:19.

1. What has the Lord promised concerning meeting your needs?

   [God has promised to provide our needs if we seek first the kingdom of God and His righteousness.]

2. Give an example from the Bible of the Lord providing for someone's needs in a supernatural way.

   [Several of the many examples of God's provision: Israel in the wilderness (Exodus 16:4-35); Jesus feeding the five thousand (Matthew 14:15-21) and the four thousand (Matthew 15:32-38); and the Lord sending ravens to feed Elijah (1 Kings 17:4-6).]

3. How does this apply to you today?

[God continues to provide for us today.]

Day Six

Read 1 Corinthians 4:2.

1. According to this verse what is your requirement as a steward?

[We are responsible to be faithful as stewards.]

2. How would you define a steward?

[A steward is a manager of another's property.]

Read Luke 16:1-2.

3. Why did the master remove the steward from his position?

[The steward was removed because he squandered the master's possessions.]

Read Luke 16:10.

4. Describe the principle found in this verse.

[If a person is unfaithful in a little matter, he or she will be unfaithful in much, and vice versa.]

5. How does this apply in your situation?

Follow-up

✔ Please write your prayer requests in your prayer log before coming to the meeting.

✔ I will take the following action as a result of this week's study:

_____

_____

_____

_____

_____

_____

_____

_____

_____

_____

_____

REMAINING AGENDA

1. _____ (10 minutes) **Play the Week 2 segment of the *Practical Application Video,* which reviews what the members are required to do for next week. Answer any questions concerning the practical application.**

   - Read the God's Part and Our Part Notes on pages 18-25 in the *Life Group Manual.*
   - Complete the Debt Homework on pages 28-31 in the *Life Group Manual.*
   - Complete the Debt List on pages 21-23 in the *Practical Application Workbook.*
   - Review Destination 2 on the *Crown Money Map.*™

2. _____ (10 minutes) **Note requests and answers to prayer in the Prayer Log.**

3. _____ (5 minutes) **End in prayer.**

REMINDER FOR LEADERS: Remember to be vulnerable with your own financial challenges. Contact each member this week and record the communication in the Care Log on page 88. Please review the mechanics of How to Conduct the Study on page 12 to confirm that you are conducting the discussion correctly.

Debt is slavery.

CROWN'S OVERVIEW OF WEEK 3: Debt is a struggle for many and is discouraged in Scripture. This week challenge the members to establish the goal of becoming debt free. Prior to attending class, the leaders should read the Debt Notes on pages 32-42 in the *Life Group Manual*.

AGENDA:

1. _____ (5 minutes) **Open in prayer.**

2. _____ (5 minutes) **Each person individually recites from memory Proverbs 22:7, TLB.**
   "Just as the rich rule the poor, so the borrower is servant to the lender."

3. _____ (5 minutes) **Confirm that members have completed the Debt List practical application and have reviewed Destination 2 on the *Crown Money Map*.™ Answer any questions concerning the practical application.**

4. _____ (80 minutes) **Begin the group discussion.**

REMINDER FOR LEADER: Do not read the Notes in class.

Scripture to Memorize

"Just as the rich rule the poor, so the borrower is servant to the lender" (Proverbs 22:7, TLB).

Practical Application

Complete the Debt List and review Destination 2 on the *Crown Money Map.*™

Day One - Let's Review God's Part and Our Part

Read the God's Part/Our Part Notes on pages 18-25 and answer:

1. How have you observed God using money to mold your character?

2. What strengths have been developed in your character?

3. What weaknesses in your character still need to be addressed?

DEBT

Day Two

Read Deuteronomy 15:4-6; Deuteronomy 28:1, 2, 12; and Deuteronomy 28:15, 43-45.

1. According to these passages how was debt viewed in the Old Testament?

    [Debt was considered a curse. Being free from debt (being a lender) was a blessing.]

2. What was the cause of someone getting in debt (needing to borrow) or being free of debt (able to lend)?

[Disobedience led to debt and obedience led to getting out of debt (being a lender).]

Day Three

Read Romans 13:8; Proverbs 22:7; and 1 Corinthians 7:23.

1. Why is debt discouraged in Scripture?

Romans 13:8 - **[We are encouraged to stay out of debt.]**

Proverbs 22:7 - **[The debtor is servant to the lender.]**

1 Corinthians 7:23 - **[We are instructed not to be slaves of men. Therefore, make every effort to get out and stay out of debt. To summarize: The Bible does not say that debt is sin, but it discourages indebtedness.]**

2. How does this apply to you personally and to your business?

3. If you are in debt, do you have a strategy to get out of debt? If you have a plan, please describe it.

LEADER— you should have approximately **one hour** of class time remaining. We recommend a three-minute stretch break for your group at this time.

Day Four

Read Psalm 37:21 and Proverbs 3:27-28.

1. What do these verses say about debt repayment?

Psalm 37:21 - **[A person who borrows but does not repay debts is called *wicked*.]**

Proverbs 3:27-28 - **[Pay debts promptly if you have the resources. Many are taught to delay repayment to use other people's money as long as possible, but this is not biblical.]**

2. How will you implement this?

Day Five

Read 2 Kings 4:1-7.

1. What principles of getting out of debt can you identify from this passage?

[We should seek the counsel of godly people, as well as the Lord's help and direction. His supernatural intervention is required whether He answers quickly, as in the case of the widow, or more slowly over time. We should use whatever resources are available—however small—in an effort to get out of debt. Involve the entire family in your effort to get out of debt.]

2. Can you apply any of these principles to your present situation? How?

Day Six

Read Proverbs 22:26-27 and Proverbs 17:18.

1. What does the Bible say about cosigning (striking hands, surety)?

Proverbs 22:26-27 - **[Do not cosign. It may cause you to lose assets you need.]**

Proverbs 17:18 - **[It is poor judgment to cosign (countersign).]**

Read Proverbs 6:1-5.

2. If someone has cosigned, what should he or she attempt to do?
[If we have cosigned, we are to humbly and diligently seek the release of our obligation.]

☑ Please write your prayer requests in your prayer log before coming to the meeting.

☑ I will take the following action as a result of this week's study:

REMAINING AGENDA

1. _____ (10 minutes) **Play the Week 3 segment of the *Practical Application Video*, which reviews what the members are required to do for next week. Answer any questions concerning the practical applications.**

   ▪ Read the Debt Notes on pages 32-42 in the *Life Group Manual*.

   ▪ Complete the Counsel Homework on pages 46-49 in the *Life Group Manual*.

   ▪ Complete the Estimated Spending Plan on pages 25-31 in the *Practical Application Workbook*.

   ▪ Complete the Spending Plan Analysis on pages 32-35 in the *Practical Application Workbook*.

   ▪ Review Destination 3 on the *Crown Money Map*.™

2. _____ **In addition to this week's *Practical Application Video* segment, be sure to use the additional video resources in the "Special Features" section of the DVD to enhance your life group.**

3. _____ (10 minutes) **Note requests and answers to prayer in the Prayer Logs.**

4. _____ (5 minutes) **End in prayer.**

REMINDER FOR LEADERS: In order to more consistently recognize God's ownership, encourage the members to continue meditating on *1 Chronicles 29:11-12*. Contact each one this week and note this in the Care Log. Remind the members to visit Crown's Web site at **Crown.org** so they can use their online tools in the "My Crown" section of Crown.org.

A wise person seeks advice.

CROWN'S OVERVIEW OF WEEK 4: Everyone should seek counsel when they need to make major financial decisions. In our culture people are discouraged from seeking counsel. The leaders should have read the Counsel Notes on pages 50-56 in the *Life Group Manual* before class.

AGENDA

1. _____ (5 minutes) **Open in prayer.**

2. _____ (5 minutes) **Each person individually recites from memory Proverbs 12:15.**

   "The way of a fool is right in his own eyes, but a wise man is he who listens to - counsel."

3. _____ (5 minutes) **Confirm that members have completed the Estimated Spending Plan and the Spending Plan Analysis practical applications and have reviewed Destination 3 on the *Crown Money Map.*™ Answer any questions concerning the practical applications.**

4. _____ (80 minutes) **Begin the group discussion.**

Scripture to Memorize

"The way of a fool is right in his own eyes, but a wise man is he who listens to counsel" (Proverbs 12:15).

Practical Application

Complete the Estimated Spending Plan and the Spending Plan Analysis, and review Destination 3 on the *Crown Money Map.*™

Day One - Let's Review Debt

Read the Debt Notes on pages 32-42 and answer:

1. Are you in debt? If so, what steps do you sense God wants you to take to become free of debt?

   [Encourage the life group members to work toward getting out of debt.]

2. What did you learn about debt that proved to be especially helpful?

COUNSEL

Day Two

Read Proverbs 12:15; Proverbs 13:10; and Proverbs 15:22.

1. What are some of the benefits of seeking counsel?

   Proverbs 12:15 – **[The person who listens to counsel is wise.]**

   Proverbs 13:10 – **[Wisdom comes to those who seek counsel, but the consequence of not seeking counsel is strife.]**

   Proverbs 15:22 – **[Plans succeed with counsel but fail without it.]**

2. What are some of the benefits you have experienced from seeking counsel?

3. What hinders you from seeking counsel?

Day Three

Read Psalm 16:7 and Psalm 32:8.

1. In what ways does God actively counsel His children?

    [The Lord does counsel His children primarily through prayer, the Bible, and godly people.]

Read Psalm 106:13-15.

2. What was the consequence of not seeking the Lord's counsel in this passage?

    [A *wasting disease* was sent because they did not seek the counsel of the Lord.]

3. Have you ever suffered for not seeking God's counsel? If so, describe what happened.

LEADER — you should have approximately **one hour** of class time remaining. We recommend a three-minute stretch break for your group at this time.

Day Four

Read Psalm 119:24; Psalm 119:105; 2 Timothy 3:16-17; and Hebrews 4:12.

1. Give several reasons why the Bible should serve as your counselor.

    [We must seek the counsel from the Word of God because it gives direction for our lives.]

Read Psalm 119:98-100.

2. Living by the counsel of Scripture —

Makes us wiser than: **[Our enemies]**

Gives us more insight than: **[Our teachers]**

Gives us more understanding than: **[Those older and more experienced]**

3. Do you consistently read and study the Bible? If not, what prevents your consistency?

Day Five

Read Proverbs 1:8-9.

1. Who should be among your counselors?

[Our parents should be among our counselors.]

2. In your opinion, who should be the number-one human counselor of a husband? Of a wife? Why?

[The husband and wife are each other's most important human counselor.]

Read Proverbs 11:14 and Ecclesiastes 4:9-12.

3. What do these verses communicate to you?

Proverbs 11:14 - **[People fail without counsel, but many counselors lead to victory.]**

Ecclesiastes 4:9-12 - **[Two or three people working together are more productive than a single individual.]**

4. How do you propose to apply this principle in your personal and/or business life?

Day Six

Read Psalm 1:1-3.

1. Whom should you avoid as a counselor?

    [Avoid the wicked as your counselor.]

2. What is your definition of a wicked person?

    [A wicked person is one who lives his or her life without regard to God.]

Read Proverbs 12:5.

3. Why should you avoid their counsel?

    [The thoughts of the wicked are not controlled by the Holy Spirit and are deceitful.]

4. Is there ever a circumstance in which you should seek the input of a person who does not know Christ? If so, when?

    [In our opinion, it is permissible to seek input from those who do not know Christ when you are gathering facts. After collecting the facts, solicit counsel from godly people before arriving at your decision.]

Follow-up

☑ Please write your prayer requests in your prayer log before coming to the meeting.

☑ I will take the following action as a result of this week's study:

REMAINING AGENDA

1. _____ (10 minutes) **Play the Week 4 segment of the *Practical Application Video,* which reviews what the members are required to do for next week. Answer any questions concerning the practical applications.**

   - Read the Counsel Notes on pages 50-56 in the *Life Group Manual.*
   - Complete the Honesty Homework on pages 60-63 in the *Life Group Manual.*
   - Complete the Snowball Strategy on pages 37-39 in the *Practical Application Workbook.*
   - Complete Debt Repayment Schedule on pages 40-44 in the *Practical Application Workbook.*
   - Complete Adjusting Your Spending Plan on pages 45-49 in the *Practical Application Workbook.*
   - Review "Things to Do Sooner Than Later" on the *Crown Money Map.*™

2. _____ (10 minutes) **Note in the Prayer Logs requests and answers to prayer.**

3. _____ (5 minutes) **End in prayer.**

REMINDER FOR LEADERS: Remember to complete the members' evaluations.

God's standard is absolute.

CROWN'S OVERVIEW OF WEEK 5: Dishonest practices are common, but the Lord demands that His children act with absolute honesty and integrity. This section is one of the most challenging of the entire study. The leaders should have read the Honesty Notes on pages 64-71 in the *Life Group Manual* before class.

AGENDA:

1. _____ (5 minutes) **Open in prayer.**

2. _____ (5 minutes) **Each person individually recites from memory Leviticus 19:11.**

   "You shall not steal, nor deal falsely, nor lie to one another."

3. _____ (5 minutes) **Confirm that members have completed the Snowball Strategy, Debt Repayment Schedule, and Adjusting Your Spending Plan practical applications, and have reviewed "Things to Do Sooner Than Later" on the *Crown Money Map.*™ Answer any questions concerning the practical applications.**

4. _____ (80 minutes) **Begin the group discussion.**

TO BE COMPLETED *PRIOR TO* WEEK 5 MEETING

Scripture to Memorize

"You shall not steal, nor deal falsely, nor lie to one another" (Leviticus 19:11).

Practical Application

Complete the Snowball Strategy, Debt Repayment Schedule, Adjust Your Spending Plan, and review "Things to Do Sooner Than Later" on the destination page of the *Crown Money Map*.™

Day One - Let's Review Counsel

Read the Counsel Notes on pages 50-56 and answer:

1. What elements of God's perspective on counsel especially interested you?

   [Encourage married couples to seek counsel from their spouses.]

2. Do you actively seek counsel when faced with a major financial decision? If not, how do you propose to do so in the future?

HONESTY

Day Two

Read Leviticus 19:11-13; Deuteronomy 25:13-16; Ephesians 4:25; and 1 Peter 1:15-16.

1. What do these verses communicate to you about God's demand for honesty?

   Leviticus 19:11-13 – **[The Lord commands us to be honest.]**

   Deuteronomy 25:13-16 – **[The Lord demands honesty in our business dealings.]**

   Ephesians 4:25 – **[We are not to lie to one another.]**

   1 Peter 1:15-16 – **[We are to be holy in our behavior just as the Lord is holy.]**

2. Are you consistently honest in even the smallest details? If not, what will you do to change?

3. What are two factors that motivate or influence us to act dishonestly?

[Some of the factors influencing dishonesty are greed, fearing that God will not provide for us, financial difficulties, and peer pressure.]

4. How does this apply to you?

Day Three

Read Exodus 18:21-22.

1. Does the Lord require honesty for leaders? Why?

[The Lord requires leaders to be honest. A major criteria for selecting leadership was honesty, because a leader will influence those under his or her authority, either for good or for evil.]

Read Proverbs 28:16 and Proverbs 29:12.

2. What are the consequences of dishonesty for people in leadership?

Proverbs 28:16 – **[A dishonest person will be removed from leadership.]**

Proverbs 29:12 – **[Subordinates will become dishonest.]**

3. How does this apply to you?

LEADER—you should have approximately **one hour** of class time remaining. We recommend a three-minute stretch break for your group at this time.

Day Four

Read Proverbs 14:2.

1. Can you practice dishonesty while fearing (respecting, honoring) God? Why?

   [No, those who practice dishonesty despise the Lord. When people are dishonest, they have concluded that God is not able to provide exactly what they need, incapable of discovering their dishonesty, and powerless to discipline them. In short, dishonest people act as if the Lord does not exist.]

Read Proverbs 26:28 and Romans 13:9-10.

2. According to these passages, can you practice dishonesty and still love your neighbor? Why?

   [No, because dishonest people hate those they hurt. However, love does no wrong to a neighbor. Because dishonesty always affects people, we cannot love and be dishonest at the same time.]

Day Five

Read Psalm 15:1-5; Proverbs 12:22; Proverbs 20:7; and Isaiah 33:15-16.

1. What are some of the benefits of honesty?

   Psalm 15:1-5 – **[More intimate fellowship with the Lord.]**

   Proverbs 12:22 – **[An honest person is a delight to the Lord.]**

   Proverbs 20:7 – **[The children of an honest person are blessed.]**

   Isaiah 33:15-16 – **[The Lord will protect and provide for the needs of the honest.]**

Read Proverbs 3:32; Proverbs 13:11; and Proverbs 21:6.

2. What are some of the curses of dishonesty?

   Proverbs 3:32 – **[A dishonest person is an abomination to the Lord.]**

   Proverbs 13:11 – **[Anything obtained dishonestly will be taken away.]**

   Proverbs 21:6 – **[Obtaining wealth by lying produces only temporary gains and eventually leads to death.]**

Day Six

Read Exodus 22:1-4; Numbers 5:5-8; and Luke 19:8.

1. What does the Bible say about restitution?

   [Restitution was required under the Old Testament law. Zaccheus is an example of a person fulfilling this obligation. Restitution involved the return of the item acquired dishonestly, plus a penalty.]

2. If you have acquired anything dishonestly, how will you make restitution?

   [Ask forgiveness from the Lord, confess your dishonesty to the one who was harmed, and make restitution. Sometimes restitution is a delicate and complex issue. The question of how to fulfill the principle of restitution should be prayerfully answered.]

Read Exodus 23:8; Proverbs 15:27; and Proverbs 29:4.

3. What does Scripture say about bribes?

   [You must never take a bribe because it will influence your judgment. The person who is not involved with bribes will live, but a leader who takes bribes will be overthrown.]

4. Have you ever been asked to give or take a bribe? If so, describe what happened.

Follow-up

☑ Please write your prayer requests in your prayer log before coming to the meeting.

☑ I will take the following action as a result of this week's study:

REMAINING AGENDA

1. _____ (10 minutes) **Play the Week 5 segment of the *Practical Application Video,* which reviews what the members are required to do for next week. Answer any questions concerning the practical applications.**

   - Read the Honesty Notes on pages 64-71 in the *Life Group Manual.*
   - Complete the Giving Homework on pages 74-77 in the *Life Group Manual.*
   - Complete Beginning Your Spending Plan on page 53 in the *Practical Application Workbook.*
   - Review the giving statement in "Prepare for the Journey" on the *Crown Money Map.*™

2. _____ **In addition to this week's *Practical Application Video* segment, be sure to use the additional video resources in the "Special Features" section of the DVD to enhance your life group.**

3. _____ **Ask students to recommend and/or contact people who might be future students. Forward any recommendations to the Crown church or city leader.**

4. _____ (10 minutes) **Note requests and answers to prayers in the Prayer Log.**

5. _____ (5 minutes) **End in prayer.**

REMINDER FOR LEADERS: Encourage those who do not yet have a current will to obtain one.

Giving is blessed.

CROWN'S OVERVIEW OF WEEK 6: Communicate the importance of giving with the proper attitude. The leaders should have read the Giving Notes on pages 78-84 in the *Life Group Manual* before class.

AGENDA

1. _____ (5 minutes) **Open in prayer.**

2. _____ (5 minutes) **Each individual recites from memory Acts 20:35.**

   "Remember the words of the Lord Jesus, that He Himself said, 'It is more blessed to give than to receive.'"

3. _____ (5 minutes) **Confirm that members have completed the Beginning Your Spending Plan practical application and have reviewed the giving statement in "Prepare for the Journey" on the *Crown Money Map.*™ Check their progress in getting a will. Answer any questions concerning the practical applications.**

4. _____ (80 minutes) **Begin the group discussion.**

Scripture to Memorize

"Remember the words of the Lord Jesus, that He Himself said, 'It is more blessed to give than to receive'" (Acts 20:35).

Practical Application

Complete the Beginning Your Spending Plan, the Spending Plan Analysis, and review Destination 3 on the *Crown Money Map.*™

Day One - Let's Review Honesty

Read the Honesty Notes on pages 64-71 and answer:

1. How does the example of Abraham (Abram) in Genesis 14:21-23 challenge you to be honest?

   [Abraham made a commitment to the Lord not to take even a thread or a sandal thong. We need to make a similar commitment to be honest, even in the smallest matters.]

2. Ask God to reveal any areas of dishonesty in your life. How do you propose to deal with these areas?

GIVING

Day Two

Read Matthew 23:23; 1 Corinthians 13:3; and 2 Corinthians 9:7.

1. What do each of these passages communicate about the importance of the proper attitude in giving?

   Matthew 23:23 – **[The Pharisees gave precisely the correct amount—a tithe of even their mint leaves. But because they gave with the wrong heart attitude, the Lord rebuked them.]**

   1 Corinthians 13:3 – **[Giving without a heart of love is of no value to the giver.]**

   2 Corinthians 9:7 – **[Do not give grudgingly or under compulsion but rather give cheerfully. The proper attitude is crucial.]**

2. How do you think a person can develop the proper attitude in giving?

[The proper attitude is the key issue in the area of giving. The only way to give out of a heart of love is to consciously give each gift to Jesus Christ Himself as an act of worship.]

3. How would you describe your attitude in giving?

Day Three

Read Acts 20:35.

1. How does this principle from God's economy differ from the way most people view giving?

[In the Lord's economic system it is more blessed to give than to receive. Most people believe the opposite.]

Read Proverbs 11:24-25; Matthew 6:20; Luke 12:34; and 1 Timothy 6:18-19.

2. List the benefits for the giver that are found in each of the following passages.

Proverbs 11:24-25 – [There is a material increase—in the Lord's time and way—to the giver.]

Matthew 6:20 – [We can lay up treasures in heaven that we will be able to enjoy through out all eternity.]

Luke 12:34 – [The heart of the giver is drawn to Christ as treasures are given to Him.]

1 Timothy 6:18-19 – [We can store treasures in heaven and *"take hold of that which is life indeed."*]

LEADER—you should have approximately **one hour** of class time remaining. We recommend a three-minute stretch break for your group at this time.

Day Four

Read Malachi 3:8-10.

1. How did God view the failure to tithe (give 10 percent)?

[The tithe was required under the law, and it was considered robbing God not to give these required gifts.]

Read 2 Corinthians 8:1-5.

2. Identify three principles from this passage that should influence how much you give.

They first gave themselves to the Lord, asking Him to direct their giving. In the same way we need to submit ourselves to the Lord when determining how much to give.]

[They were so yielded to the Lord that despite difficult circumstances they begged to give.]

[They experienced tremendous joy as a result of their sacrificial giving.]

Prayerfully (with your spouse if you are married) seek the Lord's guidance to determine how much you should give. You will not be asked to disclose the amount.

Day Five

Read Numbers 18:8-10, 24; Galatians 6:6; and 1 Timothy 5:17-18.

1. What do these verses tell you about financially supporting your church and those who teach the Scriptures?

Numbers 18:8-10, 24 – **[Godly people have always been required to participate in the maintenance of the ministry. The Old Testament believer was required to care for the place of worship and the Levites who served in the ministry.]**

Galatians 6:6 – **[Those who are taught the Scriptures should financially support their teachers.]**

1 Timothy 5:17-18 – **[God's New Testament instrument is the church, and we are to adequately support those who serve as pastors and teachers.]**

Day Six

Read Isaiah 58:6-11 and Ezekiel 16:49.

1. What do these verses say about giving to the poor?

Isaiah 58:6-11 – **[When we give to the poor, the Lord will protect us, answer our prayers, and bless us with His joy.]**

Ezekiel 16:49 – **[The primary sins of Sodom were pride and not caring for the poor, even though they had an abundance of material goods.]**

Read Matthew 25:35-45.

2. How does Jesus Christ identify with the needy?

[Jesus identifies personally with the poor. When we give to the poor, we are giving to Christ Himself. When we do not give to the poor, we are not giving to Christ, and He is left hungry and naked.]

Read Galatians 2:9-10.

3. What does this verse communicate to you about giving to the poor?

[The disciples also had a deep concern for the poor. After Paul's confirmation to minister to the Gentiles, the only counsel the disciples gave him was not to forget the poor. Think of the many issues they could have discussed. Yet, they only asked Paul to remember the poor.]

4. Are you currently giving to the needy? If not, what is hindering you?

[If your life group members do not already have a needy person in their lives, encourage them to ask the Lord to bring one.]

Follow-up

☑ Please write your prayer requests in your prayer log before coming to the meeting.

☑ I will take the following action as a result of this week's study:

_____
_____
_____
_____
_____
_____
_____
_____
_____
_____
_____
_____
_____

REMAINING AGENDA

1. _____ (10 minutes) **Play the Week 6 segment of the *Practical Application Video,* which reviews what the members are required to do for next week. Answer any questions concerning the practical applications.**

- Read the Giving Notes on pages 78-87 in the *Life Group Manual.*
- Complete the Work Homework on pages 88-91 in the *Life Group Manual.*
- Review the Spending Plan Hints on pages 97-100 in the *Practical Application Workbook.*
- Complete the Idea List on page 100 in the *Practical Application Workbook.*
- Review the "Tools for the Journey" on the *Crown Money Map.*™

2. _____ (10 minutes) **Note requests and answers to prayers in the Prayer Log.**

3. _____ (5 minutes) **End in prayer.**

Work diligently as unto the Lord.

CROWN'S OVERVIEW OF WEEK 7: Work can be one of the most fulfilling or frustrating areas of life. Our satisfaction is dependent on understanding the Lord's perspective of work. The leaders should have read the Work Notes on pages 92-100 in the *Life Group Manual* before class.

AGENDA:

1. _____ (5 minutes) **Open in prayer.**

2. _____ (5 minutes) **Everyone individually recites from memory Colossians 3:23-24.**

   "Whatever you do, do your work heartily, as for the Lord rather than for men. . . . It is the Lord Christ whom you serve."

3. _____ (5 minutes) **Confirm that members have completed the Idea List practical application, have reviewed the Spending Plan Hints, and have reviewed the "Tools for the Journey" on the *Crown Money Map*.™ Determine your members' progress in obtaining a will. Answer any questions concerning the practical applications.**

4. _____ (80 minutes) **Begin the group discussion.**

Scripture to Memorize

"Whatever you do, do your work heartily, as for the Lord rather than for men. . . . It is the Lord Christ whom you serve" (Colossians 3:23-24).

 Practical Application

Review the Spending Plan Hints, complete your Idea List, and review Tools for the Journey on the *Crown Money Map.*™

Note: Please give your leader the name of anyone who would be interested in becoming a student in a future group.

Day One - Let's Review Giving

Read the Giving Notes on pages 78-84 and answer:

1. From God's perspective it is important to give with the proper attitude. How will this impact your giving?

   [To be drawn more closely to the Lord and reap the other advantages intended for the giver, we need to give each gift to the person of Jesus Christ out of a grateful heart filled with love.]

2. What truth about giving did you learn that proved especially helpful? In what way?

WORK

Day Two

Read Genesis 2:15.

1. Why is it important to recognize that the Lord created work before sin entered the world?

   [Yes, work was instituted prior to sin entering the world. In the perfect, sinless environment of the Garden of Eden, God created work for our benefit. Work is not a result of sin and the curse.]

Read Genesis 3:17-19.

2. What was the consequence of sin on work?

   [Work became difficult as a result of sin.]

Read Exodus 20:9 and 2 Thessalonians 3:10-12.

3. What do these passages say to you about work?

   Exodus 20:9 – **[Old Testament believers were required to work six days each week.]**

   2 Thessalonians 3:10-12 – **[In the New Testament, work is also required. This verse does not recommend hunger for those who cannot work because of physical or mental limitations—only those who are capable of working but choose not to work.]**

Day Three

Read Genesis 39:2-5; Exodus 35:30-35; Exodus 36:1-2; and Psalm 75:6-7.

1. What do these verses tell us about the Lord's involvement in our work?

   Genesis 39:2-5 – **[The Lord is in control of success.]**

   Exodus 35:30-35 – **[The Lord gives us job skills and the ability to teach.]**

   Exodus 36:1-2 – **[The Lord gives us our skills and understanding.]**

   Psalm 75:6-7 – **[The Lord controls promotion and demotion.]**

2. How do these truths differ from the way most people view work?

   [The biblical perspective of God's part in work is in remarkable contradiction to the culture around us that does not acknowledge the Lord in work.]

3. How will this perspective impact your work?

   [Our work attitudes and actions should be dramatically different from those who do not recognize God's role in work. We should be humble in any of our accomplishments because God gives us skills, success, and promotion.]

LEADER—you should have approximately **one hour** of class time remaining. We recommend a three-minute stretch break for your group at this time.

Day Four

Read Ephesians 6:5-9; Colossians 3:22-25; and 1 Peter 2:18.

1. What responsibilities do the employee and employer have according to these verses?

Employee responsibilities – [Sincere obedience to employer—even one who is not good and gentle—work as unto the Lord; work heartily.]

Employer responsibilities – [The employer should serve and not threaten employees.]

2. For whom do you really work? How will this understanding change your work performance?

[We work for the Lord. This perspective will allow us to make a sincere effort—even in difficult circumstances—to serve those who are our superiors or subordinates.]

Day Five

Read Proverbs 6:6-11; Proverbs 18:9; and 2 Thessalonians 3:7-9.

1. What does God say about working hard?

Proverbs 6:6-11 – [Ants are commended for hard work and those who are lazy are warned of poverty.]

Proverbs 18:9 – [A lazy person is compared to someone who destroys.]

2 Thessalonians 3:7-9 – [Paul modeled hard work.]

2. Do you work hard? If not, describe what steps you will take to improve your work habits.

Read Exodus 34:21.

3. What does this verse communicate to you about rest?

Hard work should be balanced with adequate rest and tempered by other biblical priorities. Even during busy times, one day of rest each week was required.]

4. Do you get enough rest?

5. How do you guard against working too much?

Day Six

Read Proverbs 31:10-28 and Titus 2:4-5.

1. What do these passages tell us about women working?

Proverbs 31:10-28 – **[The excellent wife is diligent, works with her hands, acquires and prepares food, invests, provides clothes for the family, and sells merchandise. She works outside the home but always with a focus toward the home.]**

Titus 2:4-5 – **[Young wives were encouraged to be workers at home.]**

2. If you are a woman, how does this apply to your situation?

Read 2 Corinthians 6:14-18.

3. How does this concept of "yoking" or "being bound together" apply to partnerships in business and work?

[The principle of yoking applies to business partnerships. It is permissible for an employee to work for an employer who does not know Christ, but partnership with an unbeliever is discouraged.]

4. Can you give some examples from the Bible of people who retired?

[Scripture gives no example of people retiring and gives only one direct reference to retirement, which is found in *Numbers 8:24-26*. The instruction there applied exclusively to the Levites who had worked on the tabernacle.]

5. Do you think retirement, as it is practiced in our culture, is biblically acceptable? Why or why not?

[Many people retire and cease all labor to pursue a life filled with leisure. This is not biblical. We should seek to be productive as long as we are able.]

Follow-up

☑ Please write your prayer requests in your prayer log before coming to the meeting.

☑ I will take the following action as a result of this week's study:

REMAINING AGENDA

1. _____ (10 minutes) **Play the Week 7 segment of the *Practical Application Video,* which reviews what the members are required to do for next week. Answer any questions concerning the practical applications.**

   - Read the Work Notes on pages 92-100 in the *Life Group Manual.*
   - Complete the Investing Homework on pages 104-107 in the *Life Group Manual.*
   - Study the Saving and Investing section on pages 103-105 of the *Practical Application Workbook.*
   - Review the Insurance and Filing System sections on pages 105-108 of the *Practical Application Workbook.*
   - Review Destinations 4 and 5 on the *Crown Money Map.*™

   Encourage the members to continue maintaining their spending plan. Ask them to think of three creative ways to save money that would normally be spent. As the members share their ideas next week, this can be a powerful experience when they consider how steady savings grow over time.

2. _____ (10 minutes) **Note requests and answers to prayers in the Prayer Logs.**

3. _____ (5 minutes) **End in prayer.**

Consistently save.

CROWN'S OVERVIEW OF WEEK 8: This week's objectives are to learn the proper biblical attitudes toward saving and investing and to teach the scriptural framework for savings and investing. **The leaders should not recommend any specific investments or financial products or services.** Crown Financial Ministries assumes no liability for any actions taken related to specific investments or savings. The leaders should have read the Investing Notes on pages 108-116 in the *Life Group Manual* before class.

AGENDA

1. _____ (5 minutes) **Open in prayer.**

2. _____ (5 minutes) **Everyone individually recites from memory Proverbs 21:5.**

   "Steady plodding brings prosperity; hasty speculation brings poverty"
   (Proverbs 21:5, TLB).

3. _____ (5 minutes) **Confirm that members have completed the Saving and Investing and the Insurance and Filing System practical applications and have reviewed Destinations 4 and 5 on the *Crown Money Map.*™ Ensure that everyone is continuing with their spending plans. Answer any questions concerning the practical applications.**

4. _____ (10 minutes) **Ask the members to share their creative ideas on how to save money that would normally be spent.**

5. _____ (70 minutes) **Begin the group discussion.**

HOMEWORK

WEEK 8

TO BE COMPLETED <u>PRIOR TO</u> WEEK 8 MEETING

Scripture to Memorize

"Steady plodding brings prosperity; hasty speculation brings poverty" (Proverbs 21:5, TLB).

Practical Application

Complete Saving and Investing, Insurance and Filing System, and review Destinations 4 and 5 on the *Crown Money Map.*™

Day One - Let's Review Work

Read the Work Notes on pages 92-100 and answer:

1. What in the notes proved especially helpful or challenging? How will this impact you?

2. Do you usually recognize you are working for the Lord? If not, what can you do to be more aware that you work for Him?

INVESTING

Day Two

Read Genesis 41:34-36; Proverbs 21:20; and Proverbs 30:24-25.

1. What do these passages say to you about savings?

Genesis 41:34-36 - **[Joseph saved during a time of plenty to prepare for a coming famine.]**

Proverbs 21:20 - **[Those who are wise save, but the foolish only consume.]**

Proverbs 30:24-25 - **[Ants are commended as wise because they save.]**

2. If you are not yet saving, how do you propose to begin?

Read Luke 12:16-21, 34.

3. Why did the Lord call the rich man a fool?

   [The rich man was a fool because he stored up all his goods and was not rich toward God.]

4. According to this parable, why do you think it is scripturally permissible to save only when you are also giving?

   [If we save without giving, our hearts will be drawn to those possessions and away from Christ (v. 34).]

Day Three

Read 1 Timothy 5:8.

1. What is a scripturally acceptable goal for saving?

   [It is permissible to save to meet family needs.]

Read 1 Timothy 6:9.

2. What is a scripturally unacceptable reason for saving?

   [It is wrong to desire to get rich. However, it is not wrong to become rich if it is a by-product of being a faithful steward.]

Read 1 Timothy 6:10.

3. According to this verse, why is it wrong to want to get rich (refer to 1 Timothy 6:9)? Do you have the desire to get rich?

   [When we want to get rich we are actually loving money. The desire to get rich is a common attitude that can destroy our fellowship with the Lord.]

Read 1 Timothy 6:11.

4. What should you do if you have the desire to get rich?

[You should flee from this desire and pursue godly living.]

LEADER—you should have approximately **one hour** of class time remaining. We recommend a three-minute stretch break for your group at this time.

Day Four

Read Proverbs 21:5; Proverbs 24:27; Proverbs 27:23-24; Ecclesiastes 3:1; and Ecclesiastes 11:2.

1. What investment principle(s) can you learn from each of these verses, and how will you apply each principle to your life?

Proverbs 21:5 - **[Be a diligent, steady plodder and not hasty in investing.]**

Proverbs 24:27 - **[Develop your means of producing an income before buying a house.]**

Proverbs 27:23-24 - **[Know the status of your assets at all times.]**

Ecclesiastes 3:1 - **[Timing is important in investing.]**

Ecclesiastes 11:2 - **[Diversify your investments.]**

Day Five

Read Genesis 24:35-36; Proverbs 13:22; and 2 Corinthians 12:14.

1. Should parents attempt to leave a material inheritance to their children? Why or why not?

[Yes, parents should try to leave a material inheritance to their children.]

2. How are you going to implement this principle?

Read Proverbs 20:21 and Galatians 4:1-2.

3. What caution should a parent exercise?

Proverbs 20:21 - **[An inheritance should not be given into a child's care until the child is mature enough to manage the inheritance faithfully.]**

Galatians 4:1-2 - **[The appointment of a guardian through a will or trust helps ensure a child's maturity before receiving an inheritance.]**

Day Six

Gambling is defined as: *playing games of chance for money and betting.* Some of today's most common forms of gambling are casino wagering, betting on sporting events, horse and dog races, and state-run lotteries.

1. What are some of the motivations that cause people to gamble?

[People are motivated to gamble by the desire to get rich quick, by greed, and by the prospect of getting something for nothing. Many want to become wealthy so they can quit working.]

2. Do these motives please the Lord? Why?

[These motives do not please the Lord because they are contrary to His principles found in the Bible.]

Read Proverbs 28:20 and Proverbs 28:22.

3. According to these passages, why do you think a godly person should not gamble (play lotteries, bet on sporting events)?

[A person who hastens after wealth is identified as evil and will experience poverty. Please encourage your students never to bet one penny. State lotteries are particularly enticing because they have been legalized by the government and glamorized by the media.]

4. How does gambling contradict the scriptural principles of working diligently and being a faithful steward of the Lord's possessions?

[Gambling is in direct opposition to the scriptural principles of diligent work and faithful stewardship. No productive work is required in gambling; thus, a person's character is not properly developed. The odds of winning are absurdly low, and gamblers are wasting the possessions the Lord has entrusted to them.]

Follow-up

☑ Please write your prayer requests in your prayer log before coming to the meeting.

☑ I will take the following action as a result of this week's study:

_____

_____

_____

_____

_____

_____

_____

_____

_____

_____

REMAINING AGENDA

1. _____ (10 minutes) **Play the Week 8 segment of the *Practical Application Video,* which reviews what the members are required to do for next week. Answer any questions concerning the practical applications.**

- Read the Investing Notes on pages 108-116 in the *Life Group Manual.*

- Complete the Perspective Homework on pages 120-123 in the *Life Group Manual.*

- Complete Organizing Your Estate on pages 111-115 in the *Practical Application Workbook.*

- Complete the Draft a Will on pages 116-117 in the *Practical Application Workbook.*

- Review Destination 6 on the *Crown Money Map.*™

2. _____ **In addition to this week's *Practical Application Video* segment, be sure to use the additional video resources in the "Special Features" section of the DVD to enhance your life group.**

3. _____ (10 minutes) **Note in the Prayer Log requests and answers to prayers.**

4. _____ (5 minutes) **End in prayer.**

REMINDER FOR LEADER: Please recommend the members who are qualified to be future leaders. Encourage those who do not yet have a current will to get one. Remind the members to visit Crown's Web site at **Crown.org** for much more practical information on investing.

Exercise wisdom when you spend.

CROWN'S OVERVIEW OF WEEK 9: This week we will determine our God-given standard of living. In many respects, this section is the summary of the entire study. The leaders should have read the Perspective Notes on pages 124-136 in the *Life Group Manual* before class.

AGENDA:

1. _____ (5 minutes) **Open in prayer.**

2. _____ (5 minutes) **Everyone individually recites from memory Philippians 4:11-13.**

   "I have learned to be content in whatever circumstances I am. I know how to get along with humble means, and I also know how to live in prosperity. . . . I can do all things through Him who strengthens me."

3. _____ (5 minutes) **Confirm that members have completed the Organizing Your Estate and Draft a Will practical applications, have reviewed Destination 6 on the Crown Money Map,™ and are maintaining their spending plans faithfully. Answer any questions concerning the practical applications.**

4. _____ (80 minutes) **Begin the group discussion.**

Note: Think about your prayer request for the last class. It should be a "long-term" request the others can pray about when they think of you.

Scripture to Memorize

"I have learned to be content in whatever circumstances I am. I know how to get along with humble means, and I also know how to live in prosperity. . . . I can do all things through Him who strengthens me" (Philippians 4:11-13).

Practical Application

Complete Organizing Your Estate, Draft a Will, and review Destination 6 on the *Crown Money Map.*™

Note: Think about your prayer request for the last meeting. It should be a "long-term" request the others can pray when they think of you.

Day One - Let's Review Investing

Read the Investing Notes on pages 108-116 and answer:

1. What in the notes proved especially helpful?

2. Describe the specific steps you intend to take to begin saving.

PERSPECTIVE

Day Two

Read Deuteronomy 30:15-16; Joshua 1:8; and Hebrews 11:36-40.

1. What do each of these passages communicate to you about financial prosperity for the believer?

Deuteronomy 30:15-16 - **[One of the blessings of obedience was prosperity.]**

Joshua 1:8 - [**Knowing and obeying all of the commands in the Scriptures resulted in prosperity.**]

Hebrews 11:36-40 - [**Even godly people have experienced poverty and difficult circumstances while exercising faith.**]

Reflect on the lives of Job (Job 1:8-21); Joseph (Genesis 37:23-28; 39:7-20); and Paul (2 Corinthians 11:23-27).

2. Did they ever experience periods of financial abundance and at other times a lack of financial prosperity?

[**Job, Joseph, and Paul each experienced periods of plenty and times of want.**]

3. Was their lack of financial prosperity a result of sin or lack of faith?

[**Their times of poverty usually were not a result of sin or lack of faith.**]

4. Should all Christians always prosper financially? Why?

[**Once a person has fulfilled all areas of being a faithful steward, he or she is in a position for the Lord to prosper him or her financially. However, the Lord may not for one of three reasons: (1) He is building our character (Romans 5:3-4); (2) He needs to discipline us in areas of our lives where there is sin (Hebrews 12:6,10); and (3) God's sovereignty (Hebrews 11:36-40).**]

Read Psalm 73:1-20.

5. What does this passage tell you about the prosperity of the wicked?

[**The psalmist questioned why the wicked prospered. He was envious. Godliness did not seem to "pay off." Then the Lord revealed the wicked person's end: sudden, eternal punishment.**]

Day Three

Read Philippians 4:11-13 and 1 Timothy 6:6-8.

1. What do these passages say about contentment?

Philippians 4:11-13 - [**Contentment is not something that occurs naturally; it is learned. We can learn to be content in any circumstance.**]

1 Timothy 6:6-8 - [**Godliness with contentment is a means of great gain. We cannot take anything with us when we die, and we should be content with our basic needs satisfied.**]

2. How does our culture discourage contentment?

3. How do you propose to practice contentment?

LEADER—you should have approximately **one hour** of class time remaining. We recommend a three-minute stretch break for your group at this time.

Day Four

Read Matthew 5:25-26 and Romans 13:1-7.

1. Does the Lord require us to pay taxes to the government? Why?

   [The Lord requires us to pay taxes because He has instituted government to serve people. The consequence of tax evasion is punishment.]

Read James 2:1-9.

2. What does Scripture say about partiality (showing favoritism)?

   [Do not show favoritism to the wealthy. It is a sin to be partial.]

3. Are you guilty of partiality based on a person's financial, educational, or social status?

Read Romans 12:16 and Philippians 2:3.

4. How do you plan to overcome partiality?

   [Be of the same mind toward each person and consider each person as more important than yourself.]

Day Five

Read Acts 4:32-37 and 1 Thessalonians 4:11-12.

1. What do these passages communicate to you about lifestyle?

   Acts 4:32-37 - **[An equality of needs being met within the body of Christ led to revival.]**

   1 Thessalonians 4:11-12 - **[We are encouraged to live quiet, industrious lives.]**

2. How do the following factors influence your present spending and lifestyle?

   Comparing your lifestyle with that of friends and other people -

   Television, the Internet, magazines, catalogs, and other advertisements -

Your study of the Bible –

Your commitment to Christ and to things that are important to Him –

3. Do you sense that the Lord would have you change your spending or your standard of living? If so, in what way?

Day Six

Read Deuteronomy 6:6-7; Proverbs 22:6; and Ephesians 6:4.

1. According to these passages, who is responsible for teaching children how to handle money from a biblical perspective?

   [It is the responsibility of the parents. Introduce the concept of establishing a strategy for independence—the goal of having each child independently managing his or her finances (with the exception of food and housing) by the senior year in high school.]

2. Stop and reflect for a few minutes: Describe how well you were prepared to manage money when you first left home as a young person.

   [Most children leave home ill-equipped to manage money.]

3. Describe how you would train children to:

   Create and maintain a spending plan –

   Give –

   Save –

   Spend wisely –

Follow-up

☑ Please write your prayer requests in your prayer log before coming to the meeting.

☑ I will take the following action as a result of this week's study:

_____

_____

_____

_____

_____

_____

_____

_____

REMAINING AGENDA

1. _____ (5 minutes) **Play the Week 9 segment of the *Practical Application Video,* which reviews what the members are required to do for next week.**

   - Read the Perspective Notes on pages 124-136 in the *Life Group Manual.*
   - Complete the Eternity Homework for Week 10 on pages 140-143 in the *Life Group Manual.*
   - Complete the My Life Goals on pages 119-125 in the *Practical Application Workbook.*
   - Complete the Involvement and Suggestions Survey on Crown.org.
   - Review Destination 7 and Long-Term Goals on the *Crown Money Map.*™

2. **Ask the members to be thinking about a "lifetime" or "long-term" prayer request for next week. Also ask each one to write a letter to his or her pastor, describing the benefits of the study, because this will encourage the church leadership.**

3. _____ (5 minutes) **Answer any questions concerning the practical applications.**

4. _____ (10 minutes) **Note in the Prayer Logs requests and answers to prayers.**

5. _____ (5 minutes) **End in prayer.**

REMINDER FOR LEADERS: Prepare the Certificates of Achievement for the members who have been faithful.

INSTRUCT THE MEMBERS to complete the Involvement and Suggestions Survey online in the "My Crown" section of Crown.org. The input from the members is very important for the continued improvement of this study.

All will give an account.

CROWN'S OVERVIEW OF WEEK 10: This section deals with God's view of our time on earth and eternity. To summarize, life on earth is short and eternity is forever. How we use our time, talents, and money will impact eternity. Leaders should have read the Eternity Notes on pages 144-151 in the *Life Group Manual* before class.

AGENDA

1. _____ (5 minutes) **Open in prayer.**

2. _____ (5 minutes) **Everyone individually recites from memory Mark 8:36.**

   "What does it profit a man to gain the whole world, and forfeit his soul?"

3. _____ (5 minutes) **Confirm that the members have completed the My Life Goals practical application, have reviewed Destination 7 and Long-Term Goals on the *Crown Money Map*,™ and have completed the Involvement and Suggestions Survey. Ensure that they are continuing to maintain their spending plans and have executed a current will. Answer any questions concerning the practical applications.**

4. _____ (80 minutes) **Begin the group discussion.**

TO BE COMPLETED PRIOR TO WEEK 10 MEETING

Scripture to Memorize

"What does it profit a man to gain the whole world, and forfeit his soul?" (Mark 8:36).

Practical Application

Complete My Life Goals and review Destination 7 and Long-Term Goals on the *Crown Money Map.*™

Also, complete the Involvement and Suggestions Survey in the "My Crown" section of Crown.org.

Day One - Let's Review Perspective

Read the Perspective Notes on pages 124-136 and answer:

1. What was the most helpful concept you learned from the notes?

2. Do you sense the Lord would have you alter your lifestyle in any way? If so, in what way?

ETERNITY

Day Two

Read Psalm 39:4-6 and Psalm 103:13-16.

1. What do these passages say to you about the length of life on earth?
   [Life on earth is short.]

Read Psalm 90:10, 12.

2. Why did Moses ask God to teach us to number our days?

[Numbering our remaining days on earth helps us realize the brevity of our lives. Understanding this, we are better able to make wise decisions on how to use our time and money.]

3. Estimate the number of days you have left on earth. How does this impact your thinking?

4. Based on your number of days, what actions will you take?

Day Three

Read 1 Chronicles 29:15; Philippians 3:20; and 1 Peter 2:11.

1. What do these passages say about your identity on earth and in heaven?

    1 Chronicles 29:15 - **[We are aliens, strangers, and sojourners on earth.]**

    Philippians 3:20 - **[We are citizens of heaven, which is our real home.]**

    1 Peter 2:11 - **[We are strangers on this earth.]**

Read 2 Peter 3:10-13.

2. What will happen to the earth?

[The earth and everything on it will be totally destroyed.]

3. How should this impact the way you invest your time and spend money?

LEADER—you should have approximately **one hour** of class time remaining. We recommend a three-minute stretch break for your group at this time.

Day Four

Read Ecclesiastes 12:13-14 and 2 Corinthians 5:9-10.

1. What will happen to each of us in the future?

    Ecclesiastes 12:13-14 - [**The Lord will judge all our deeds, even those we think are hidden.**]

    2 Corinthians 5:9-10 - [**All of us will stand before the judgment seat of Christ and give an account of our actions.**]

Read 1 Corinthians 3:11-15.

2. How would you describe the works (give some examples) that will be burned at this final judgment?

    [**Any of our actions done out of what the Bible calls "the flesh"—apart from submission to Christ as Lord. Anything done out of pride or with improper motives.**]

3. Give some examples of works that will be rewarded.

    [**The smallest action, when done to glorify Christ, will be rewarded. In** *Matthew 10:42* **the Lord tells us that even giving someone a cup of cold water shall be rewarded.**]

4. What are you doing that will survive this final judgment?

Day Five

Read 2 Corinthians 4:18.

1. What does this verse say to you?

    [**What we see will last only a relatively short period of time. The things we cannot see will last forever and should be of primary importance.**]

2. As you reflect on eternity, answer this question thoughtfully: What three things do I want to accomplish during the rest of my life?

3. What can I do during my lifetime that would contribute most significantly to the cause of Christ?

4. In light of these answers, what actions or changes do I need to make?

Day Six

Read the Eternity Notes on pages 144-151 and answer:

1. What was the most important concept you learned from reading the notes?

2. Please complete the Involvement and Suggestions form online in the "My Crown" section of Crown.org.

3. Describe what has been the most beneficial part of the *Biblical Financial Study* for you:

Follow-up

☑ Please write your prayer requests in your prayer log before coming to the meeting.

☑ I will take the following action as a result of this week's study:

REMAINING AGENDA

1. _____ (10 minutes) **Play the Week 10 segment of the *Practical Application Video*.**

2. _____ (5 minutes) **Award the Certificates of Achievement to those who successfully completed the course.**

3. _____ (5 minutes) **Take long-term prayer requests and note them on the Prayer Logs.**

4. _____ (5 minutes) **Leaders pray for each member individually.**

REMINDER FOR LEADERS: We suggest you write each member (or couple) an encouraging letter or e-mail, summarizing what you appreciate most about them. May God richly bless you in every way for serving others.

"Pray for one another. . . . The effective prayer of a righteous man can accomplish much"
(James 5:16).

PRAYER LOGS

ALWAYS PRAY

Be faithful in prayer.

"Pray for one another" (James 5:16).

Name _____   Spouse _____

Home phone _____   Children (ages) _____

Business phone _____   _____

Mobile phone _____   _____

E-mail _____   _____

Home address _____   _____

_____   _____

Week	Prayer Request(s)	Answers to Prayer
1		
2		
3		
4		
5		
6		
7		
8		
9		
10	*My long-term prayer request:*	

"Pray for one another" (James 5:16).

Name _____   Spouse _____

Home phone _____   Children (ages) _____

Business phone _____   _____

Mobile phone _____   _____

E-mail _____   _____

Home address _____   _____

_____   _____

Week	Prayer Request(s)	Answers to Prayer
1		
2		
3		
4		
5		
6		
7		
8		
9		
10	*My long-term prayer request:*	

"Pray for one another" (James 5:16).

Name _____ Spouse _____

Home phone _____ Children (ages) _____

Business phone _____ _____

Mobile phone _____ _____

E-mail _____ _____

Home address _____ _____

_____ _____

Week	Prayer Request(s)	Answers to Prayer
1		
2		
3		
4		
5		
6		
7		
8		
9		
10	*My long-term prayer request:*	

"Pray for one another" (James 5:16).

Name _____ Spouse _____

Home phone _____ Children (ages) _____

Business phone _____ _____

Mobile phone _____ _____

E-mail _____ _____

Home address _____ _____

_____ _____

Week	Prayer Request(s)	Answers to Prayer
1		
2		
3		
4		
5		
6		
7		
8		
9		
10	*My long-term prayer request:*	

"Pray for one another" (James 5:16).

Name _____ Spouse _____

Home phone _____ Children (ages) _____

Business phone _____ _____

Mobile phone _____ _____

E-mail _____ _____

Home address _____ _____

_____ _____

Week	Prayer Request(s)	Answers to Prayer
1		
2		
3		
4		
5		
6		
7		
8		
9		
10	*My long-term prayer request:*	

"Pray for one another" (James 5:16).

Name _____   Spouse _____

Home phone _____   Children (ages) _____

Business phone _____   _____

Mobile phone _____   _____

E-mail _____   _____

Home address _____   _____

_____   _____

Week	Prayer Request(s)	Answers to Prayer
1		
2		
3		
4		
5		
6		
7		
8		
9		
10	*My long-term prayer request:*	

"Pray for one another" (James 5:16).

Name _____ Spouse _____

Home phone _____ Children (ages) _____

Business phone _____ _____

Mobile phone _____ _____

E-mail _____ _____

Home address _____ _____

_____ _____

Week	Prayer Request(s)	Answers to Prayer
1		
2		
3		
4		
5		
6		
7		
8		
9		
10	*My long-term prayer request:*	

"Pray for one another" (James 5:16).

Name _____   Spouse _____

Home phone _____   Children (ages) _____

Business phone _____   _____

Mobile phone _____   _____

E-mail _____   _____

Home address _____   _____

_____   _____

Week	Prayer Request(s)	Answers to Prayer
1		
2		
3		
4		
5		
6		
7		
8		
9		
10	*My long-term prayer request:*	

"Pray for one another" (James 5:16).

Name _____   Spouse _____

Home phone _____   Children (ages) _____

Business phone _____   _____

Mobile phone _____   _____

E-mail _____   _____

Home address _____   _____

_____   _____

Week	Prayer Request(s)	Answers to Prayer
1		
2		
3		
4		
5		
6		
7		
8		
9		
10	*My long-term prayer request:*	

"Pray for one another" (James 5:16).

Name _____ Spouse _____

Home phone _____ Children (ages) _____

Business phone _____ _____

Mobile phone _____ _____

E-mail _____ _____

Home address _____ _____

_____ _____

Week	Prayer Request(s)	Answers to Prayer
1		
2		
3		
4		
5		
6		
7		
8		
9		
10	*My long-term prayer request:*	

Member Evaluation

REQUIREMENTS	NAMES						
WEEK 1 ATTENDANCE							
SCRIPTURE MEMORY							
PRACTICAL APPLICATION							
HOMEWORK							
WEEK 2 ATTENDANCE							
SCRIPTURE MEMORY							
PRACTICAL APPLICATION							
HOMEWORK							
WEEK 3 ATTENDANCE							
SCRIPTURE MEMORY							
PRACTICAL APPLICATION							
HOMEWORK							
WEEK 4 ATTENDANCE							
SCRIPTURE MEMORY							
PRACTICAL APPLICATION							
HOMEWORK							
WEEK 5 ATTENDANCE							
SCRIPTURE MEMORY							
PRACTICAL APPLICATION							
HOMEWORK							
WEEK 6 ATTENDANCE							
SCRIPTURE MEMORY							
PRACTICAL APPLICATION							
HOMEWORK							

WEEK 7

WEEK 8

WEEK 9

WEEK 10

It is important to track the performance of your life group members to determine who is faithful in their attendance, Scripture memory, practical application, and homework. Place an "x" in the appropriate box to indicate faithfulness, and leave it blank if they were not faithful in that particular area. An electronic version of this form is available in the "My Crown" section of Crown.org.

Care Log

Leaders: _____ _____

Beginning Date of Life Group Study: _____

Week	Initials of leader responsible for contact ⬇	LIFE GROUP MEMBERS							
1									
2									
3									
4									
5									
6									
7									
8									
9									
10									

Description of first social activity (approx. Week 5):

Description of second social activity (approx. Week 10):

We want to hear from you!

- Did you enjoy this study?
- What kind of impact did it have in your personal finances?
- Did your financial outlook improve during the study?
- Did this study meet your expectations?
- Do you have any suggestions for improving the study?

After you have completed this life group study, would you take a few minutes and share your personal comments, suggestions, and stories with us? We sincerely value your input as we strive to make our resources better.

Log in to the "My Crown" section of Crown.org, log in as a Life Group Leader, and look for the "Involvement and Suggestions" link. Your comments are confidential and will only be used to improve this study.

Thank you in advance for your willingness to share your experience in this study with us!

Starting Your Journey to True Financial Freedom

Welcome!

We are so glad you have decided to take the journey to True Financial Freedom!

So, what is True Financial Freedom?

God has a special purpose for your life. And He doesn't want anything to prevent you from fulfilling the purpose for which you were created. True Financial Freedom is knowing that God owns it all, finding contentment with what He provides, and being free to be all He made you to be.

The *Crown Money Map*™ was created so that you can achieve this life-changing freedom. And we want to help you every step of the journey!

How to use your *Crown Money Map*™

Before you begin the 7 steps to true financial freedom, complete the following important steps. When these are completed, identify where you are on the *Crown Money Map*™ and begin your exciting journey!

My Life Purpose

Describe what you believe is your life purpose. Your purpose is similar to gas in a car. It should be the fuel that drives you to the destination of True Financial Freedom. It's the motivation that propels you.

Prayerfully consider what matters most to you. Consider your relationship with God, with your family and friends, and your service to others. What is your passion? Now summarize your life purpose.

If there is a Bible verse that captures your life purpose, write it down to serve as your guide.

My Life Goals

Goals are the steps you will take to accomplish your life purpose. Divide your goals into short-term and long-term objectives. Now you know what you need to accomplish to reach your life purpose.

Tools for the Journey

Crown has identified outstanding tools designed to help you safely reach each destination of your trip. These practical tools have been used successfully by millions of people.

012008

MY LIFE PURPOSE

What do you want your life to count for? How do you want to be remembered? What do you believe God created you to be? As you think about describing your life purpose, consider these important areas of your life—the Lord, your family and friends, and others.

Describe your purpose as it relates to—

My relationship with God _____
_____

My relationship with my family and friends _____
_____

My service to others _____
_____

Summary of life purpose:
_____
_____
_____
_____
_____

If there is a Bible verse that communicates my life purpose, this is it:
_____
_____
_____
_____
_____

MY LIFE GOALS

These should be action statements that help you achieve your life purpose. Your goals should be simple and measurable. Your short-term goals should be accomplished within a year.

Short-Term Goals

God _____

Family and friends _____

Service to others/ministry _____

Financial (Income, Debt, Savings, Investments, Giving, Spending)
_____

Career/Skills _____

General _____

Long-Term Goals

God _____

Family and friends _____

Service to others/ministry _____

Financial (Income, Debt, Savings, Investments, Giving, Spending)
_____

Career/Skills _____

General _____

FRAGILE

FREEDM